It's Only a Matter of Time

even though time, as such, does not exist

Flloyd Kennedy

Liverpool

Flloyd Kennedy
Liverpool, Merseyside, UK.
www.flloydkennedy.com

Book Layout © 2017 BookDesignTemplates.com
Cover design

It's Only a Matter of Time/ Flloyd Kennedy. -- 1st ed.
ISBN **978-1-8381946-4-2**

Dedication to Owen, Natalie, Aurelia and the next one,
because they will know what to do

"the profoundly anarchic spirit at the basis of all poetry"

–ANTONIN ARTAUD

Contents

An Origin Story
for Natalie

In the beginning
there was a whale
big and blue and beautiful
perfectly big
beautifully blue
Alone in an ocean of nothing.
Or so it seemed.

And in the beginning
there was a universe
so infinitesimally, illogically small
that no impossibly large whale
could ever know, or understand
why, or where it might be.
And the universe floated
alone in the ocean of nothing.
Or so it dreamed.

The whale moved in perfect peace
throughout the silent void
blissfully unaware of the presence
of the infinitesimally tiny universe
sleeping, perfectly at rest
within its still, silent
lack of being
anything more

than being
infinitesimally
small.

So into the lacking of light
that signified nothing
but freedom to move
swam the whale.
And its tail began to swish
back and forth
and the sound was
perfectly swishy
if illogical because
what was there
to swish against?
Nothing but perfectly
nothing. And yet—

The whale heard the sound
and something stirred inside its heart.
Its great mind registered
a feeling,
a sensation that grew from a tiny
tickle to a wave of recognition
that its perfect body
with its perfect tail
had created something
out of nothing—

out of nothing but itself.
Out of nothing
but itself
and the nothingness
of the void.

And the sound shimmied
around its body and fluttered
across its fins.
It brushed past its nose
as it turned and tumbled
through the darkness,
till the tickle became a giggle
and the giggle grew into a guffaw
and the guffaw gurgled and gushed
out of the whale's giant mouth
in a rhythmical pattern
that merged with the swishing
and slowly, elegantly,
the whale created song.

And as the whale swam
and its tail swished
the veil of nothing
began to shift
and the whale sang
and its heart lifted
feeling resistance
a form of insistence

that nothing was moving
while everything changed.

And somewhere, somehow
from the deepest depths of its
infinitesimally tiny beingness,
the universe felt a shiver
a shock of a shake
and it began to crack and to creak
and to cleave in two.

And the whale
swam through
and the song shivered
and shook each piece apart
till a river of universal
smithereens
smashed themselves
into being
as a glowing
unknowing
festive flowing
showing itself
in the trail of a whale.

So it was that the whale swam on
and sang on.
And in its wake were left
the makings of galaxies

with planets and stars
meteors and matter that is
and isn't (as far as can be seen)
there at all.

On and on the whale sings
and swims,
swishing its tail
fluttering its fins,
rejoicing in the sound of its voice,
never looking backwards
because there is no back or forth
no south or north
no up nor down
no in or out
in the endless nothing that is
and is not—nothing.

And still the whale takes enormous pleasure
in bringing into being
the stuff of the universe
The universe which forms
and endlessly reforms
all the while tirelessly yearning
to return
to its once upon a time
infinitesimally
tiny, dream of itself.

limericks to live and laugh by

In the year of twenty-twenty two
I shall bite off more than I can chew
When it's all masticated
And I'm constipated
There'll be such a Hullabaloo.

In the year of twenty-twenty two
Sun will shine, sky will be blue
Optimism's outrageous
And mildly contageous
But at least half the time, 'twill be true.

In the year of twenty twenty-two
I'll continue to do what I do
Writing plays that end badly
Podcasts that end madly
And even a poem or two.

In the year of twenty twenty-two
There'll be peace in the world through and through
And the climate will stay
As it was yesterday
As the piggies fly into the blue.

Falling and rising

Sitting at my desk (aka my dining table),
watching a film on the tv set
on the table because it is also
the monitor for my computer,
wondering why it is still day.
Will the night ever fall?

Does night ever fall?
Or does it rise?
Does the darkness that envelops me
as the sun sweetly sinks—
does the darkness simply arrive?
Slowly, softly grading the sky
To greyness
making it harder to see
the detail of a chaotically charmed life.

O what a day

The Sun is shining far away
as it always does.
Only today
it's buzzing
blue above my head
waiting to be fed
with clouds of hope and
possibilities.
They'll rain on my parade
with the force of all I've ever lost
and everything I've ever yearned for
showering me and splashing me
with dreams
in droplets
of feverish delight.

Roll Over

a song

Over and over and over again
rolling along 'cross the watery main
traversing continents, mountain and plain
and all for the sake of variety.

Who'd be a traveller, wandering far
from home and hearth, by train or car
abandoning friends to follow a star
whose provenance hints at dubiety?

Only a wanderer, born and bred
accustomed to rocking and rolling ahead
pausing only to share and to shed
accumulations of property.

If a rolling stone gathers no moss
and a roller coaster loses its gloss
can a life habituated to loss
become part of a stable society?

Too many questions, answers none.
Guess I'll keep rolling until I'm done.
Over and over as long as there's fun
with a minimal loss of propriety.

Rolling over and out on the tide,
hoping to land on the other side
of the biggest wave I'll ever ride
then roll over in perpetuity.

Over and over and over again
rolling along 'cross the watery main
traversing continents, mountain and plain
and all for the sake of variety.

Use your brain

a song

Use your brain. Use your brain
It sits in your head
and it waits in vain
for you to use it.
Don't abuse it
It's the only one you've got
and you need it, quite a lot.

It's the only one you've got
and you need it— quite a lot

Use your mind. Use your mind
It lives with your brain
and if you don't find
a way to use it—think about it!
You just might lose it.

Cos your mind is your brain
if you only knew it.
Stir it or flavour it,
simmer it or stew it,
It comes up with stuff—
you might think it's fluff
but fluff can turn to silk
if you work with it enough.

And Silk is a thread
like those thoughts in your head
that you weave into fantasies
of horror and delight.
Twist them or knot them
as long as you've got them
there's no need to be concerned
that they'll turn out alright.

They know what to do.
It's not up to you.
Your job is to nourish them
with goodness so they'll flourish.

So use your brain
to feed your mind
Give it some space
to search and find
Some elegant tropes
made of silken ropes
You won't be sorry.
You'll be in a hurry
To do it again,
and again and again,
And never, no never to cause it pain.
(Don't do that)

Use your brain. Use your brain
It sits in your head

and it's happy to contain
the mind that
notices and feels
all that life has to reveal.
So choose to use it.
Don't abuse it—
It's the only one you've got
And you need it, quite a lot.

It's the only one you've got
And you need it—quite a lot

Today's the day

Today is the day
I will finally sort myself out.
I know...
I said that last time.
And I will probably say it again.

So today is the day
I will finally start
to sort myself out.

I've been thinking about it
for so long,
It's time I put it into words.
Words out loud.
There is something about
saying things out loud
that seems to make them...
Happen.
So.
Here goes...

What has shifted?
Forgive the young woman
who held back.
Give her space.
Accept her.

Get over her.
Be ok with your wee shards of pottery.
Play with them.

Recycle them.
Waste not, want not.
That's what our parents used to say to us.
At least, mine did.
Were they so unusual?
When did it become a thing
to be wasteful?
When did we begin to notice
That wastefulness was unsustainable?
At least, some of us did.

What is it, exactly
that we want to sustain?
Life, as we know it, Jim?
The way of life we somehow have
persuaded ourselves that we always had?
The way of life we somehow have
come to believe is our 'human right'?

And another thing...

What, exactly, do we mean by
Sustainability?
What do I mean by Persuasion?
What do you mean by Belief?

In transit

I am addicted to turning points
Bridges - half way across
neither here nor there
Lifts - that point of no return
between floors.
Or passing through new towns,
places never seen before.

The transit lounge provides comfort
when I'm neither here nor there.
Always looking for the edge
always peeping round the corner
always pausing at the border
leaning back, but crossing over
Nevertheless.

The highway beckons
till the roundabout looms large
suggesting one more reckoning
to be resolved
sooner rather than later.
Plagued by restlessness.
mistaking the cross road
for the roundabout

Poised on a knife-edge
or balancing on the point of a pin
Lockdown provided both time and space
to let myself down from the high wire
forego the balancing act
"Should I stay or should I go?"

Ode to the hot flush (or flash, if you must)

There's nothing Homeric about hormones
and there's nothing chimeric about chemistry.
Why should there be?
Nothing but sounds, combinations of sounds
that differ both subtly and profoundly
in their frequencies.

There is nothing normal about normalcy
It's a word that cries out for diplomacy.
Flush or flash, bosh or bash, it's a matter of fash—
ion, or culture or social contingency.

Word playing won't cure the discomfort
any more than reduce the embarrassment
just for a moment, an instant, a jiffy.
It might hold you intact as you pass the experience
enough to remember that life will go on.
Your face will retain its blotched insistence
on telling the world what your hormones have done
Even though they've long gone
back to their balanced—
not-balanced existence.

There's nothing much placid about a placebo.
There's nothing hap-hazard about a gazebo.

There's no sense in nonsense
No lice in license
No Inns in incense
No men in menses
No verse in controversy.

But word play can help to dim the pain
and keep you sane
when all else that you've tried
has been in vain.

No Pets Allowed in a Spaceship

It's just as well I'm on my own.
Without a cat.
Although perhaps it is
because I'm on my own
that when a sadness strikes me
like a sudden non-infectious
(no you cannot catch it)
virus
it surges from some hidden depths
beyond my conscious
ability to control
and bursts between my lips—
that unbidden "mmmmmiaow..."

And it's just as well that
I don't have a dog.
Although if I did—
have a dog—
for one thing, I'd be fitter
stronger, within and without.
I don't need a dog, because
whenever a pathetic anguish
strikes me, without warning
from within, it erupts in an
manner worthy of the most
loveable labrador who,

in sight of the last morsel of gristle
sliding into the bin from my plate
before her tensile tongue (
slip it down her greedy
gullet,
howls the howl of the
most bereft
benighted woebegone
beast of the forest.
Urrrrooooo!

It's just as well. Because
if I did, have a cat, or a dog,
they would, almost certainly
jump ship, at the first hint of a whimper.
And so it is, that I can rest assured
in the secure knowledge that
no-one can hear my abandoned
miaou, or urooo
floating far above the panic
in my virtual pandemic-inspired
space capsule.

I Finished a Book

I finished a book!
(You finished a book?
What's the big deal?)
I finished a book! A whole real book.
A book in my hand
(that rhymes with grand)
made of paper and ink
(That rhymes with think)
Coz a book in the hand is worth
Ten Thousand Trillion
on a screen
(that rhymes with scream).
No it doesn't.

Her name is...

Her name is... gosh, what was it again?
Oh, sorry, I know it's something unusual...
Also known as... that woman who does stuff
It's a boy's name, but not really - and
She comes from Australia, I think...
but she keeps on moving.
She used to be younger
She knows she is... much older
She wants to be someone
whose name you'd remember
She wishes she could make fantastic
Stuff that you'd remember
She needs to do more stuff.
She has absolutely no idea
how to stop moving about,
Even though she thinks she has.
She loves that people ask her to do stuff
She hates that it's never quite
professional enough
for her totally unrealistic ideals
She's happy that the stuff she does is good stuff
Her name is totally forgettable, in spite of –
or because of -
the fact that she is the only one who has it.
And that's all that matters.

Screensaver I
first born son with paternal grandmother

Pixels flicker on the screen
focus, to reveal you
my first born
curled at ease
confident within the soft curve
of your grandmother's arms
eyes tentatively
absorbing the warmth
of a late autumnal sky
lips apart to greet the taste of
your sweet breath
flooding deeply to feed
the blood that fires your will
your playful spirit
warming the muscles
that will engage you in
games of comradeship
and challenges of study
then take you halfway
round the world
where you will love
and grow your own
babies, imprinting your
curiosities within their
sturdy individualities
supporting their burnishing

ambitions as you strive
to clear the way through
hazardous times
that they may thrive
and grow as you have done
into maturity
your once golden hair
now speckled with grey
behind the spectacles distinguishing
the care and precision you bring
to everything you touch
extending yourself to accomplish
with patience the life
you've earned till now—
And O!
How I long to hold my baby still.

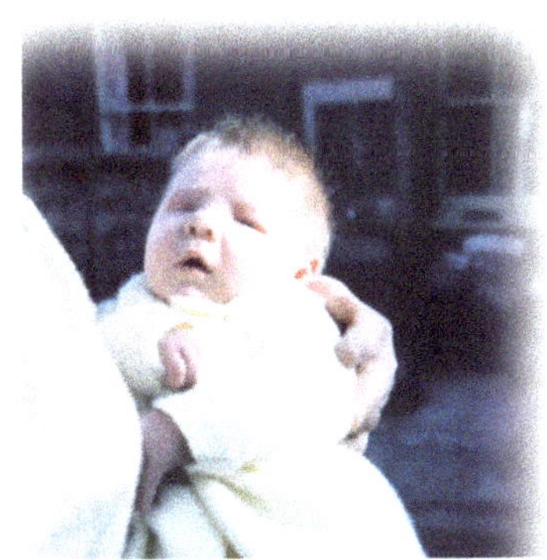

Screensaver II
maternal grandmother with my two sons

Snapped with a 'proper' camera
by the side of the Crinan canal
on your first visit to meet your grandchildren
and I need to know that my boys are safe.
This morning I dreamt that the sea was wild
and a barber shop was open by the shore
and you insisted on going in
and one of the barbers was kind,
and he trimmed the top of your head
over the plastic pandemic screen
and I excused myself politely and flew
like a raging Valkyrie over the sand
to the trembling waters
for I needed to know that my boys were safe.
And in the photo you stand,
grandly angelic,
your arms spread behind them,
angling two shyly smiling cherubs
into your care
but you weren't there for me.
Half my life ago, that moment
filled me then with resentment
for lack of the love
I never knew you felt for me.
But time was kind
and I have grown to know

although I'll never understand
the choices you had made.
The photograph reveals the power
you concealed to care for us,
the care you took to keep us safe
which broke us,
the love you never shared
which made us,
and I will always need my two boys to know
that I need them to be safe.

Screensaver III
second son with his new-born daughter

You walk with quiet pride
down the hospital corridor
towards your new life as a father
clasping the carrier handle
away from your body
Mandalorian-like ushering out

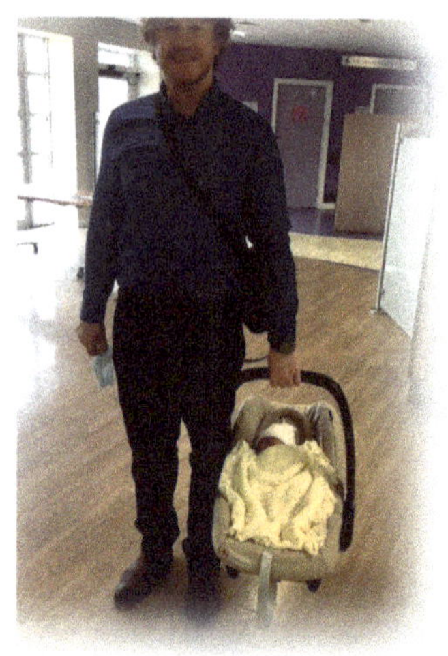

into the world
the tiny person
who holds the secret
power of your genes
within each cell
in her body
and she will bless you
challenge you
fight you
define you
as you and your brother
have defined me.

Screensaver IV
Skype call with Mercer Is.

The screenshot has been cropped
stripped of the framing data
so that you could all have been
on the other side of the table
the kids poking funny faces
because I said "Don't pose!"
You had turned away
to ensure they had quality
Grandma time; but
glancing back to see them
on the screen, you
smiled, and in the background
their mother's arm flung skyward
with laughter.

Screenshot V

Family gathering: Aigburth, Picton and Mercer Is.

Three windows
Into three worlds apart
tricking into a shared memory
trapping our faces
looking and seeing
each other in a new light.
Two brothers laughing
and I laughed more
for the joy of holding you both
safe in that moment on the screen
because I cannot hold you both
In my arms
not at once
not any more
not until the screen dissolves
and time revolves
to place us in one place
a space to relish skin
and unmediated voices safely.
And I still need to know my two boys are safe.

Walking on Tiree—Gale Force 8

How strong the wind would have to be
before we would be deterred
from donning our anoraks
our boots and gloves and woolly hats
tipping the wee one into the pushchair
grabbing the hand of the not quite so wee one
setting off on a grand adventure
wanderlust with sand whipping our noses.
As long as our eyes were clear
we walked, and took turns
to steer the baby, or gambol about
before and behind and
O, we forgot the dog!
Back we go, her joyful jumping
gleefully avoiding
the confining catch of the lead.
So we walk and let her run free
with the wind in her ears
and her tail whiplashing
its own miniature gale.
We'll stop at Auntie Doris's—
But no, the dog is almost halfway
down the road to Skye Mary's
head full of visions of the collies
rushing down the pathway
yapping their welcome.

And so we follow sheepishly
with extra effort now, the wind
catching at our voices
tossing our calls to 'Stop!' and 'Stay!'
back in our faces.
But then she does. At the roadside
with never a car or a tractor in sight
she sits and waits
her tiny frame trembling with the effort
then leads us safely across.
There is tea and warm scones
and a good blather
before scampering home
with a tailwind
In half the time.

Responding to the BBC

"We need to know you're out there,"
Said the man on the radio.
I'm out here, I replied—inside.

But really, I'm in here.

And you, man on the radio—
you lie.
You have no actual need.
I know if I reply
You will not read
What I say.
You may
Cast across the air waves
Words gifted you from a few
Souls who bravely contact you
To share one tiny aspect of their lives.
Not mine, though.

I'll stay inside,
playing hide
and seek with the world
that swirls beyond my walls.
My insides can contain
chaotic machinations of my brain

And I'll surprise myself by framing
the nonsense into lines

of pixels that combine
to form these words upon the screen.
My fingers work much better
than my eyes at making letters
congeal into phrases
holding sense in sentences,
forcing gaps between unwarranted
intentions so that slowly
the low-lying
untruths that grow with monstrous power
fed by the lack of balance
in my brain chemistry
can be trained into structured
conscious language.

This is fact.

And I'm still here.

Who is with me?

Who can see, as 1 can
with eyes in my ears
the horror, stark unyielding
wall of latent anguish?

1 am no voice in the wilderness,
crying a prophesy of God-given vengeance.

My voice is not a voice, it is a mind,
a thought crying out in my head.
The thought is a solid crowbar
that batters the walls of my skull
denting, chipping, crumbling,
gaining strength with each blow
fed each day on the fearful
mindless fodder of words.
Words cannot translate my thought.
It is a monster which belies description.
And so I wonder -
are my words
the true translation of my thoughts?

Who is with me?
Am I alone in my possession
of this wordless thought?
It echoes tramping feet.

Quick rhythm.
How quick? How many feet?
How can a sound reverberate
through sixty years of life, death,
love, loss, science and
time.
That history could be re-enacted
is irrelevant.

That it will be re-enacted
is inevitable.

A fishy story

Standing behind the sea wall,
grey sky
warm
bunch of kids
scattered over the pebbles.
"Do you want a go?"

I can't believe he means me
but I jump at the chance anyway.

Length of fishing line
an old rusty hook.

"Throw it out. Further!"

I throw, awkward. Sit. Wait.
Seagulls.
A bus trundling by
squeaky brakes.
The line goes taut!

"I've got one."
"Show me," the boy tries to help.
"I can do it!"

The kids gather.

Silence.
The line suddenly goes slack.
I pull it up.
I know by the weight
there's something.

The boy laughs. What?
I pull.
The other children laugh.

"It's a crab!"

I'm thrilled.
A crab is still good.
You can eat a crab.

The boy grabs the line.

"I'll do it."

I'm grateful.
It's so exciting
I caught it
all by myself
but I don't want to
mess with hooks.

Splash.

Where is it?

"Where's my crab?"

"You don't want a crab,"
says the boy.

I am devastated.
I wanted that crab.
I could have eaten that crab.
I could have taken that crab home with me.

"Mum! I caught a grab.
Really. I did.
A crab. It was a little crab
but I caught it.
And that boy threw it back
in the ocean."

My sister: "Where it is then?
Where's the crab?"

My mother says: "Quiet please, girls,
I've got a headache."

"Caught a crab, did you?
You never did.
You didn't catch anything."
"Did so. He threw it back."

"Who? What boy?
I didn't see any boy.
You didn't catch anything."
"I did. I caught it,
all by myself!"

"Girls! I'm warning you!"

(quietly) "Liar"
"Not."
"Yes you are. Little liar.
"Not."
"That's it!" (Smacks all round)

"That's not fair!
She started it."
"I did not! I didn't do anything at all."
"You did! you said—"

"I don't care who started it!!!
You're both doing it.
Enough!"

(SILENCE)

Dad didn't believe me either.

40

How to wear a face mask, if you want to extend a pandemic

A song

I wear my mask on my chin
That way I get to breath in
All the wonderful air
That surrounds me everywhere
I'm invincible

The air's so fresh and clean
You always know where it's been
There's not a virus to be seen
You know what I mean
it's invisible

And if I can't see it,
it doesn't exist
It cannot hurt me
But if you insist
That I wear a mask
I'll wear it on my wrist
Or around my neck
Or—my personal twist
Hanging from one ear
Don't tell me to desist
Or that it's risible!

I wear my mask on my chin
That way I get to breath in
All the wonderful air
That surrounds me everywhere
I'm invincible

My mouth may be hidden
Under cotton or linen
But my nose must be
Constitutionally free
That's irrefutable.

I do not need to be jabbed
That leaves holes in my skin
And as everyone knows
That's how the germs get in
My DNA is my own
It's as pure as the mist
And the more you nag me
The more I'll resist
It's reprehensible

I wear my mask on my chin
That way I get to breath in
All the wonderful air
That surrounds me everywhere
I'm invincible

But it can't be denied

That mask wearing has been tried
Not by everyone, of course,
I refuse to endorse that-
coz we aren't all the same
I have the right to choose
There's always someone else to blame
So I've nothing to lose
When it all goes wrong again.
That's indisputable.

I wear my mask on my chin
That way I get to breath in
All the wonderful air
That surrounds me everywhere
I'm invincible

Do not aspire to perfection

Do not aspire to perfection.
Or rather, do not expect to attain perfection.
And if you ever
believe
you have achieved it
understand that you have already lost
your sense of perspective.
An aspiration is something to be worked towards.
The implied motion is forwards
There is a destination to be reached
an assignation with a greatly desired
achievement. A goal, so to speak.
Score!!!
And then—what?
Do it again?
Or aspire to something else?
Anything is possible
if it can be imagined.
As long as the imagined desire
is not perfection, in and of itself.
Perfection is not a station where you alight.
It is a bridge to be crossed.
Perfection is innately unattainable.
Perfection requires the ability to dance
on the head of a pin.

It is — if it is anything at all —
impermanent. A transitory state.
Essentially unsustainable.

We humans all have flaws,
loose threads in our seams.
That's how we grow.
One apparently perfect
earthenware pot
cannot expand
it cannot learn
or know its raison d'etre,
or give birth,
or replicate itself.
No.
It is perfect,
as far as perception allows.
It is finished.
All it can do now
Is be — gin to decay.

Yet it is not without purpose.
It still has the capacity to be
More than its oh so
apparently perfect form.
And when we flawed,
imperfect creatures
perceive that perfect pot
all our cracks and flaws

will shift
to realign our limitations
allowing room for us to
fill ourselves with wonder
awe, desire, envy
ambition or despair.

Sometimes all of the above.

And should we seal those cracks,
conceal those flaws
reveal a perfectly repaired veneer
we find ourselves bound, locked
inside a state of stasis
with no power to change
no freedom to move either
ourselves, or others.
As we stand in awe
before that perfect pot
what we experience is e-motion.
Our perception of the pot
sends us outwards
with the potential
for growth, for learning
expanding our horizons.
We realise that there is more to us
with our flaws and imperfections
than perfection could ever offer.

And I will come and go
and make mistakes as I do so.
For I am a cracked vessel
with the possibility of motion,
and of transformation.

And even if I break in half
each half still holds a life
in the process of transition.
And if I live my life
in a state of transition
That is a way of life.
And each half is only one way of life.
But the other half of the cracked vessel
is a different way.
And so I need to accept myself
beyond the cracks.

And if the vessel were to shatter
Into many parts
uneven, jagged or rounded,
smooth or sharp
each separate fragment
still informs the whole,
retains the memory of the shape
it once contributed to.
And each single fragment
will acknowledge
its responsibility

to continue
in its new and separate life
as well as its responsibility to hold—
something.
One tiny fragment
might not hold much water.
It might not be able to carry
enough food to
feed a family.
Yet still it holds the right
to continue
the life cycle
of the original vessel
of which it is still a vital part.

In the beginning,
the universe was dark.
Possibly.
And then it was light.
Probably.
And then—think about it!
It cannot stay light forever
no matter how much it might suit you,
or me.
It does not belong to you,
or to me.

Paradoxically, the universe is perfect.
Perfectly transitioning between light and dark

expansion and contraction
motion and stillness.
Each instant of its existence
is perfectly what it is
in that unsustainable instant.
It is constantly changing
and consistently complete.
What it was and what it is
and what it will be
only retains significance
for us
inasmuch as we are part of it.

And so we also are already perfect.
There is no other perfection to aspire to.

Perfection,
 therefore
is not a solid state.
It is not a destination
patiently waiting to be arrived at.
It is not a valid goal.
Achievements, goals, destinations
are merely staging posts along the way—
signposts that prove we are alive.

To be alive is to be constantly in motion.
Actually, to be dead is not the end of motion.
Our cells, our energy,

our worth have simply moved on
with the endless
(as far as we are capable of understanding it)
e-motion of the universe itself.

Do not aspire to perfection.
You will always be disappointed
whether you believe you have achieved it
or not.
Understand its transitionary nature.
Strive to get close enough to glimpse it
and do not stop there.
Keep moving.
Something beyond that vision of perfection
is waiting to inspire you.

2photo courtesy James Wafer

Flloyd Kennedy, Liverpool-based, Australian-born actor, singer-songwriter, performance poet, director and voice/speech/accent coach, took part in the British folk revival in the late 1960s, performed street theatre, cabaret and fringe theatre in Scotland throughout the 1980s and 90s, established Golden Age Theatre to tour contemporary and classic theatre throughout Scotland. She returned to Australia in 1997 where she undertook research into the performing voice (specifically Shakespeare) for her doctorate. Back in the UK since 2015, Flloyd teaches voice and acting skills at colleges and universities in the UK, US and Australia, currently teaching online through her private studio Being in Voice and she regularly performs at online Open Mic spoken word and music events. In non-pandemic times she tours her solo verse plays with music around the world.

In 2021 Flloyd began writing, performing and producing weekly vignettes, glimpses into the life of a fictitious old woman as she negotiates her life and declining faculties through the 21st century. It is broadcast as a podcast audio drama, "Am I Old Yet?" on all major podcasting apps, and also via the website https://amIoldyet.com.

Flloyd has two sons, four grandchildren, one grand dog, two grand kittens, and is a proud member of Equity.

Also by Flloyd Kennedy
BOOKS

Sunsets & Kites

scatterings of light and dark in poems, songs and essays

Home is Where I Hang My Pot

poems fierce and gentle, from somewhere over the hill

"funny, wonderfully anarchic and bonkers" *Jane Vicary*

"the real deal: honest, unsparing, hilarious and heartfelt. Her wryly observed stories, told in poetry and song" *Lauren Grodstein*

"Flloyd's book is a blockbuster, get in there for a nice present or something to cuddle up with these dark winter months" *George Melling*

"I found all the poems and stories entertaining and thought provoking, and some of them I'll go back and read again - and possibly again!" *Mabel Macarthur*

"There is a slowness in this that is missing in the world. A kindness. A gentle beauty to the words and rhythms that allows the deeper meanings to move in the shadows" *Ted Gray*

(available in paperback, eBook and audiobook)

Shish Mahal Cook Book

compiled by Flloyd Kennedy

Alloway Publishing, Ayr 1982

all proceeds to the Prince & Princes of Wales Hospice, Glasgow.

"A lovely little gem. I've tried a few recipes from this book with gr8 success. The chicken dhansak is very tasty but to be fair they all nice. I would recommend this book whatever your ability is on the curry ladder."

"Fantastic recipes, who would have thought those delicious onions you get with your pappadums are marinated in ketchup! Best Indian recipe book ever (and I do have other Indian cookbooks now)."

PERFORMANCE

The View from Over the Hill

(preview performance)

is available on Youtube at https://youtu.be/qXlTtWEigVE

MUSIC

Flloyd's songs are available online as singles from

Bandcamp

https://flloydwith2ells.bandcamp.com/

also Spotify, Apple Music, Google Play, Amazon Music

and all major music streaming sites.

www.ingramcontent.com/pod-product-compliance
Lightning Source LLC
Chambersburg PA
CBHW050045040726
47599CB00015B/1802